# *In the* PRESENCE *of* GOD

## Find Answers to the Challenges of Life

# Dr. CREFLO A. DOLLAR

**WARNER Faith®**

NEW YORK  BOSTON  NASHVILLE

Unless otherwise indicated, all Scripture quotations are taken from the *King James Version* of the Bible.

Scripture quotations marked NAS are taken from the *New American Standard Bible*. Copyright © The Lockman Foundation 1960, 1962, 1963, 1968, 1971, 1972, 1973, 1975, 1977. Used by permission.

Scripture quotations marked AMP are taken from *The Amplified Bible, Old Testament*. Copyright © 1965, 1987 by Zondervan Corporation, Grand Rapids, Michigan. Used by permission.

Warner Books Edition
Copyright © 2000, 2004 by Dr. Creflo A. Dollar
Creflo Dollar Ministries
2500 Burdette Road
College Park, GA 30349
All rights reserved.

Warner Faith

Revised in 2006

Time Warner Book Group
1271 Avenue of the Americas, New York, NY 10020
Visit our Web site at www.twbookmark.com.

Warner Faith® and the Warner Faith logo are trademarks of Time Warner Book Group Inc.

Printed in the United States of America

First Warner Faith Edition: March 2006
10  9  8  7  6  5  4  3  2  1

LCCN: 2005937852
ISBN-13: 978-0-446-69843-6
ISBN: 0-446-69844-X

# Contents

# *Introduction*

"What are the benefits?"

This is one of the first questions you are likely to hear after offering someone a job. The fact is, we are living in a benefit-oriented society with everyone wanting to know, "What's in it for me?"

Most people don't seem to realize they are missing a greater source of benefits than they can possibly imagine: the benefits that come from living and abiding in the presence of Almighty God.

Everything you could ever want or need can be found in the presence of the Lord.

Do you need healing? You'll find it in His presence.

Do you need provision? You'll find it in His presence.

Every good thing anyone could possibly desire is waiting in the presence of a loving, holy God. It's so simple. Yet so many believers miss this powerful truth.

It's a truly amazing concept when you stop and think about

it. The God of the universe, that awesome Being who spoke the worlds into existence, has given you and me the opportunity to walk into His throne room and fellowship with Him.

Even more amazing is that many Christians fail to exercise this wonderful privilege! Think about it. Every day, countless believers make the decision to say no to God's offer of fellowship, choosing instead to spend their time filling their minds with television, gossip, or mindless recreation.

Many have searched high and low for answers to their problems, never thinking to seek them at the feet of God. They have consulted pastors, counselors, psychologists, psychiatrists, gurus, and self-help books. They have been to seminars, workshops, retreats, and advances. All this time the answer has been waiting for them—waiting in the presence of the Lord.

God's Word offers us practical keys to abiding in the presence of the Lord. That's what this book is about: gaining an understanding of how we can move into and remain in the presence of God.

When we learn to do that, then and only then will the answers and solutions you are looking for be found. It is then that you will begin to enjoy the benefits of God's presence.

I once heard a preacher make a statement that seemed to resonate in my spirit. She said very bluntly, "To not live in daily contact with God is not only sinful; it's stupid."

There is a mountain of truth in that statement. There is so

much to be gained from learning to walk in God's presence, and there is so much we miss when we neglect it. The good news is, the Bible has much to say about *how* to live in the presence of God. But before we dive into the Scriptures, let's begin by defining the term *presence of God*.

First of all, to be present obviously means to be in or at a certain location. During school days, when you heard the teacher call your name during the roll call, you answered by saying, "Present."

What does it mean to be in the presence of God? Does it mean we can see Him with our natural eyes or hear Him speak to us in an audible voice? Probably not. We can, however, experience the presence of God on several different levels.

One of the most basic and most powerful ways to experience the presence of God is through His Word. You may be thinking, *How can I experience God by reading a book?* Let me show you. Look at John 1:1:

> *In the beginning was the Word, and the Word was with God, and the Word was God.*

God and His Word are inseparable. When you are in the presence of the Word, you are in the presence of God. There is something powerful that happens when you open that Book and spend quality time in it. Something happens in your heart. Reading the Word feeds your spirit, and that Word continues to work in you and change you even after you have closed the Book and walked away.

Of course, spending time in the Word isn't the only way to experience God's wonderful presence. Another obvious way is by spending time in prayer, particularly when you pray God's Word.

There is a big difference between praying God's Word and praying some dry, lifeless, traditional prayer. So much doubt, unbelief, and religiosity is prayed by Christians who simply don't know any better. They will pray like this:

> *Our dear, kind, heavenly Father, we are Your humble, no-good, undeserving servants. We beseech Thee to stop by just for a little while. We know we're nothing but miserable worms—just wicked sinners saved by grace—but if You could give us a little crumb off Your table, we'd be satisfied, Lord.*

This kind of prayer is not acceptable to God. It may sound humble to the religious mind, but it is 100 percent contrary to the Word of God. The Bible says if you are born again, you have been made the righteousness of God in Christ Jesus and a joint-heir with Jesus Christ. (2 Cor. 5:21; Rom. 8:17.)

The false humility that characterizes so many religious prayers could not be more unbiblical. If you want to pray prayers that will usher you into the presence of God, don't pray religion; pray God's Word.

Of course, there are other ways to experience God's presence. Helping you understand how to benefit from them is what this book is all about. For you to understand what it's like to truly experience God's presence, you have to go back to the beginning.

*In the*
# PRESENCE
*of*
# GOD

1

# *Going Back to the Beginning*

ASK YOURSELF THIS question: How much of God's presence does He want us to experience?

There is only one way to accurately answer that question. We must go to the one place in the Bible where things on earth were exactly as God intended them to be: the Garden of Eden.

Let's go back now to the beginning and discover God's intent for man and his fellowship with his Maker.

## *Man's God-Given Dominion*

In Genesis 1:26, we find these words:

> And God said, Let us make man in our image, after
> our likeness: and let them have dominion over the fish
> of the sea, and over the fowl of the air, and over the

*cattle, and over all the earth, and over every creeping thing that creepeth upon the earth.*

I think it is significant that the first thing God gave man was dominion, or authority. In other words, God wanted to create a partner in ruling the earth. In making man, God duplicated Himself in the sense that Adam became "god" of the earth, just as He (God) is God of the universe.

Now I realize this is a controversial statement for some people, but I have never quite figured out why. The Scripture is clear on this subject. Still, some people get quite offended when you use the term "god" when referring to man.

Even translators of the *King James Version* of the Bible fell into this trap. When translating Psalm 8:4–5, they chickened out of making a literal translation. This Scripture reads:

> *What is man, that thou art mindful of him? and the son of man, that thou visitest him?*
> *For thou hast made him a little lower than the angels, and hast crowned him with glory and honour.*

The word translated *angels* in the above passage is the Hebrew word *elohim*.[1] According to *Strong's Exhaustive Concordance*, in most Old Testament Scriptures where you see the word *God*, it is translated from the Hebrew word *elohim*.[2] In fact, *elohim* is used in Genesis 1:26: "And God [*elohim*] said, Let us make man in our image. . . ."

Yet in this case the translators of the *King James Version* chose instead to render it *angels*. Why? Because their natural minds simply could not grasp the reality of what God was saying there. The translators of the *New American Standard Bible*, however, got it right. This version says:

> *What is man, that Thou dost take thought of him? And the son of man, that Thou dost care for him?*
> *Yet Thou hast made him a little lower than God, and dost crown him with glory and majesty!*
>
> Psalm 8:4,5 NAS

Man wasn't created lower than the angels. The Word clearly states that angels are here to render service to God's people.

> *Are they [the angels] not all ministering spirits, sent forth to minister for them who shall be heirs of salvation?*
>
> Hebrews 1:14

God created man just a notch below Himself and, according to the passage we just read from the *New American Stan-*

*dard Bible*, intended him to be crowned "with glory and majesty."

When you begin to get a clear picture of the authority and dominion God intended man to walk in, you can see how much our thinking has been corrupted by religion. But authority was not the only thing God gave man in the Garden.

*stop here 8·20·12*

## The Breath of Life

In Genesis 2:7, we find a remarkable passage of Scripture:

> *And the Lord God formed man of the dust of the ground, and breathed into his nostrils the breath of life; and man became a living soul.*

Can you picture this scene? God took some dust from the earth and formed a slab of flesh. Then He breathed His life into that flesh. What a moment that must have been! God, the eternal Creator of heaven and earth, breathed into man the very thing which makes God be God.

This kind of life referred to in the New Testament—eternal life, the life Jesus has—is in the original Greek language *zoe*,[3] which means "life"—the God-kind of life. The uniqueness of who God is was transferred from God into that slab of flesh, ". . . and man became a living soul."

I want you to notice how, at that moment, man had the presence of God inside him in the form of God's *zoe* life.

That presence gave man supernatural ability in every area of existence. He was gifted physically, intellectually, and spiritually.

## When God Comes to Visit

As we have seen, God's nature and ability was present *inside* Adam in the form of God's *zoe* life. But that was not the only level at which Adam enjoyed the presence of God. As we are about to see, man experienced God's presence in a much more literal way.

In Genesis 3:8, we find God "walking in the garden in the cool of the day" looking for Adam and Eve. Obviously it was God's practice to spend time with them in this way on a regular basis.

Think about that. Adam and Eve had the privilege of walking, talking, laughing, and fellowshipping with God—face to face! They experienced the presence of God in the fullest way you can possibly imagine.

The reason this is so hard for most of us to comprehend is that, even though we are born-again children of God, we still carry around the old sin-consciousness. Even though the Word says we are righteous and justified and sanctified by the blood of Jesus, we are still more sin-conscious than righteousness-conscious.

Prior to falling into sin, do you think Adam and Eve greeted God's presence in the Garden with fear, shame, or a sense of unworthiness? Absolutely not! They greeted Him with joy and a total sense of belonging.

It was only after sin had stripped them of their innocence and covering of glory that they felt unworthy to enjoy God's presence.

If you want to know what you can expect from dwelling in the presence of God, take a look at what Adam experienced. Above all else, he experienced an abundant provision for every need he could possibly have.

In Genesis 2:9, we see God providing an abundance of food:

> And out of the ground made the Lord God to grow every tree that is pleasant to the sight, and good for food. . . .

In verses 11 and 12, we see Him providing wealth:

> The name of the first [river] is Pison: that is it which compasseth the whole land of Havilah, where there is gold;
>   And the gold of that land is good. . . .

Then in verse 18, we see Him providing companionship and completion:

> And the Lord God said, It is not good that the man should be alone; I will make him an help meet for him.

Are you beginning to get the picture? When you live in the presence of God, no needs will go unmet. Abundance, sufficiency, and increase are all you will ever see.

The presence of the Lord is a wonderful thing. Not only do you, as a child of God, get to experience the wonderful fellowship and communion of God Himself, you get all your needs met as a side benefit. That's why Jesus was able to say:

> But seek ye first the kingdom of God, and his righteousness; and all these things shall be added unto you.
>
> Matthew 6:33

When you find the kingdom of God, you have found God's presence. When you have found God's presence, you can know that every need will be met in abundance.

## Running from the Presence

An awareness of sin will cause you to shrink from the presence of God. That is precisely what we see happening to Adam and Eve after they were seduced by Satan and had rebelled against God.

Look at Genesis 3:8–10:

> And they heard the voice of the Lord God walking in the garden in the cool of the day: and Adam and his

7

*wife hid themselves from the presence of the Lord God*
*amongst the trees of the garden.*

*And the Lord God called unto Adam, and said unto*
*him, Where art thou?*

*And he said, I heard thy voice in the garden, and I*
*was afraid, because I was naked; and I hid myself.*

Adam and Eve's disobedience stripped them of their covering of glory. It also stripped them of their ability to stand in God's presence with no sense of shame. That is one of the most devastating things about sin: it robs you of your confidence before God.

*For if our heart condemn us, God is greater than our*
*heart, and knoweth all things.*

*Beloved, if our heart condemn us not, then have we*
*confidence toward God.*

1 John 3:20,21

What a tragic thing to have had the privilege of walking and fellowshipping with God, and then to throw it away for a lie. The good news is, Jesus—the last Adam—came to restore that privilege to you and me. The problem is, many Christians don't seem to be able or willing to exercise that privilege.

That's what this book is all about: discovering God's plan to restore you and me to His presence.

In the coming chapters we will continue to explore God's Word and discover keys to enjoying the benefits of God's presence. As we have seen by looking at God's original plan for creation, it is in His presence that all our needs are met in abundance.

## Claim Your Benefits!

What is man, that Thou dost take thought of him? And the son of man, that Thou dost care for him? Yet Thou hast made him a little lower than God, and dost crown him with glory and majesty!

Psalm 8:4,5 NAS

## My prayer in the power of the Word . . .

_____

_____

_____

_____

_____

_____

_____

## Study Questions

1. If someone asked you, "How much of God's presence does He want us to experience?" what would you say?

_____

_____

_____

_____

_____

2. How do you experience God's presence in your life?

_____

_____

_____

_____

_____

3. What do you think God wants from each of us?

_____

_____

_____

_____

_____

4. How does sin disrupt our relationship with God?

_____

_____

_____

_____

_____

# 2

# *Walking with God*

As we learned in chapter 1, Adam and Eve forfeited their right to enjoy the presence of God when they committed high treason against Him. Until then, they had the privilege of walking with God in the cool of the day. After the Fall, they were banished from the Garden and from God's refreshing presence.

This does not mean, however, that no one ever walked with God again. In fact, in Genesis 5 we find an interesting footnote in the genealogy of Adam regarding his descendant Enoch:

> *And all the days of Enoch were three hundred sixty and five years:*
>
> *And Enoch walked with God: and he was not; for God took him.*
>
> Genesis 5:23,24

Many preachers and theologians have speculated about what was meant by these words in verse 24: "And Enoch walked with God. . . ." There have been many different theories on this subject. I personally don't think it is any great mystery. To walk with God simply means to obey Him and keep His commandments.

In Enoch, God found a man He could entrust with His presence. Enoch was a man who would obey God. We know something else about Enoch: he was a man of faith. How do we know that? God's Word tells us so in Hebrews 11:5–6:

> **By faith Enoch was translated** that he should not see death; and was not found, because God had translated him: for before his translation he had this testimony, that **he pleased God.**
>
> **But without faith it is impossible to please him. . . .**

Doesn't that tell you something? After Adam fell, God started looking for a man He could fellowship with, a man He could walk with in the cool of the day. He finally found one when He found a faith man—a man who would take God at His Word and obey it.

God is looking for the same kind of people today. His eyes are searching to and fro throughout the whole earth for men and women who will live by faith and obey His Word. These are the people He wants to walk with, the people He wants to bless.

## Caught Away

I want you to notice something else about Enoch. As we read in Genesis 5:24: *"And Enoch walked with God: and he was not; for God took him."*

Enoch never died. He never left a body behind to be buried and decay. His walk of fellowship with God was so strong that one day the Lord came for a visit and Enoch just went home with Him when they were done. He simply disappeared from the face of the earth!

Although Enoch was the first man in history to be taken up to heaven without dying, he certainly was not the last.

In the book of Second Kings, we find another man who walked with God: Elijah, the prophet. In chapter 2, we see God sending down a chariot of fire to pick up Elijah and carry him to heaven. Once again, a man who knew intimate fellowship with God was whisked away without tasting the sting of death. (v. 11.)

I am firmly convinced that we are living in a day when we will see the same thing again, only this time on a much larger scale. I believe we are the generation of believers who will one day, in the twinkling of an eye, be snatched up to heaven to be with the Lord. This event is called the Rapture.

*For the Lord himself shall descend from heaven with a
shout, with the voice of the archangel, and with the
trump of God: and the dead in Christ shall rise first:*

*Then we which are alive and remain shall be caught
up together with them in the clouds, to meet the Lord
in the air: and so shall we ever be with the Lord.*

1 Thessalonians 4:16,17

I am also convinced that not every person who calls himself "Christian" will be making this glorious trip. Many religious folks are in for the shock of their lives when they discover that their church membership or American citizenship is not enough to qualify them for the Rapture.

But for those who are walking with God, walking in obedience to His Word and fellowshipping with Him, that day will hold nothing but joy.

## A Place of Refuge

Enoch had a great-grandson named Noah. Not too many years after Enoch's disappearing act, Noah discovered another one of the prime benefits of walking with God: protection.

In Noah, God found a man who would walk in obedience and faith. According to Genesis 6:9:

*These are the generations of Noah: Noah was a just man and perfect in his generations, and Noah walked with God.*

In Genesis 6:22, we read:

*Thus did Noah; according to all that God commanded him, so did he.*

Noah's close walk with God resulted in him and his entire family being saved from the destruction of the Flood. It also resulted in the preservation of the human race.

The same will be true for God's people today. A great tribulation is about to come upon the earth; but if you will walk with God, you will be spared. The ark of Jesus will carry us above the wrath and destruction that is about to be unleashed upon mankind.

There is protection in the presence of God.

## Claim Your Benefits!

By faith Enoch was translated that he should not see death; and was not found, because God had translated him: for before his translation he had this testimony, that he pleased God.

But without faith it is impossible to please him.

Hebrews 11:5,6

### My prayer in the power of the Word . . .

_____

_____

_____

_____

_____

_____

_____

## Study Questions

1. What does it mean to walk with God?

_____

_____

_____

_____

_____

2. Describe someone you know who walks with the Lord.

_____

_____

_____

_____

_____

3. When have you walked with God?

_____

_____

_____

_____

_____

4. What is the result of walking with God?

_____

_____

_____

_____

_____

# 3

# *"Show Me Your Glory!"*

IN THIS STUDY, we are on a journey through the Bible in search of revelation concerning the presence of God. Our next stop on this journey takes us to the tabernacle of Moses.

Few men in history have experienced the presence of God to the degree that Moses did. He experienced God in the burning bush. He experienced Him in the miraculous plagues on Egypt. He experienced Him in the fire and thunder on Mount Sinai. And he experienced Him in the tabernacle. (Ex. 3:2–6; ch. 8–11; 19:16–18; 25:8,9; 33:7–23.)

The tabernacle of Moses is actually a type or foreshadowing of the God-man Jesus. Whereas in Moses' time God dwelt in the tent of the tabernacle, under the New Covenant God dwelt in a house of flesh—the body of Jesus of Nazareth. Even more astounding, the presence of God can now dwell within you and me!

## God's Presence Manifested

There is much truth we can glean from an understanding of the tabernacle of Moses. Let's take a look at how the presence of the Lord was manifested there:

> And it came to pass, as Moses entered into the tabernacle, the cloudy pillar descended, and stood at the door of the tabernacle, and the Lord talked with Moses.
>
> Exodus 33:9

The "cloud" accompanying the presence of the Lord is a common occurrence in the Old Testament. Why was this cloud so consistently linked to God's manifest presence? Because it was necessary to protect fallen man from the pure presence of God.

Fallen, sinful man cannot survive in the pure presence of God. The Lord, in His love and mercy, sent the cloud to protect Moses. But even with a cloud between them, the relationship between Moses and God was an extraordinary one. Read on:

> And the Lord spake unto Moses face to face, **as a man speaketh unto his friend.** And he turned again into

*the camp: but his servant Joshua, the son of Nun, a*
*young man, departed not out of the tabernacle.*

*And Moses said unto the Lord, See, thou sayest*
*unto me, Bring up this people: and thou hast not let me*
*know whom thou wilt send with me. Yet thou hast said,*
*I know thee by name, and thou hast also found grace*
*in my sight.*

*Now therefore, I pray thee, if I have found grace in*
*thy sight, shew me now thy way, that I may know thee,*
*that I may find grace in thy sight: and consider that this*
*nation is thy people.*

*And he said, My presence shall go with thee, and I*
*will give thee rest.*

*And he said unto him, If thy presence go not with*
*me, carry us not up hence.*

Exodus 33:11–15

Did you catch this exchange between God and Moses? God said to him, "My presence shall go with thee." In response, Moses was saying, "That's good, Lord, because if Your presence doesn't go with me, I don't want to go!"

Moses understood something about the presence of God that most believers today don't. He knew God's presence was the only thing that would carry them all the way through to the Promised Land. He had the wisdom to realize that without the power and provision which comes from abiding in God's presence, he might as well not even try to walk down the block, much less walk through the wilderness.

## *"I Want More!"*

One thing I have noticed about the presence of God: it whets your appetite for more. Spend a little time in God's presence and soon you won't be satisfied with just a little taste now and then. You will want more of the sweetness of His presence. More of His power. More of His glory.

That's what happened to Moses. Look at Exodus 33:18:

> *And he [Moses] said, I beseech thee, shew me thy glory.*

Moses was no longer satisfied to fellowship with God from the middle of a dense cloud. After he had experienced a little of God's glorious presence, he wanted more! He was saying, "Get this cloud out of the way, Lord! I want to see Your glory! I want to see Your face!"

Did God reject Moses' request and rebuke him for being so presumptuous? No!

God will always be just as eager for your fellowship as you are for His—even more so. Remember, it was God who set Adam in the Garden to be able to enjoy close, intimate com-

munion with Him. It was man who put up the wall of separa-
tion between the two of them.

God will always grant you fellowship and revelation to the
degree that you can handle it without being harmed. Look at
how God responded to Moses' request to see His glory:

> And he said, I will make all my goodness pass before
> thee, and I will proclaim the name of the Lord before
> thee; and will be gracious to whom I will be gracious,
> and will shew mercy on whom I will shew mercy.
>
> And he said, Thou canst not see my face: for there
> shall no man see me, and live.
>
> And the Lord said, Behold, there is a place by me,
> and thou shalt stand upon a rock:
>
> And it shall come to pass, while my glory passeth by,
> that I will put thee in a clift of the rock, and will cover
> thee with my hand while I pass by:
>
> And I will take away mine hand, and thou shalt see
> my back parts: but my face shall not be seen.
>
> Exodus 33:19–23

That cleft in the rock is a foreshadowing of the ultimate
Rock, Jesus. (1 Cor. 10:4.) It is in Him that we are able to experience God's goodness and glory.

## *Full Circle*

We see Moses and the cloud of glory one more time on the stage of history. Nearly 2,500 years after the events we just read about, another remarkable event occurred. We read about it in Matthew, chapter 17.

> *And after six days Jesus taketh Peter, James, and John his brother, and bringeth them up into an high mountain apart,*
>
> *And was transfigured before them: and his face did shine as the sun, and his raiment was white as the light.*
>
> *And, behold, there appeared unto them Moses and Elias talking with him.*
>
> *Then answered Peter, and said unto Jesus, Lord, it is good for us to be here: if thou wilt, let us make here three tabernacles; one for thee, and one for Moses, and one for Elias.*
>
> *While he yet spake, behold, a bright cloud overshadowed them. . . .*
>
> Matthew 17:1–5

Once again we find Moses on a mountain in the midst of a cloud. But this time something is different. This time God is present on the earth in human flesh. Peter, James, and John had been looking into Jesus' face for months. They had even

26

touched Him! God had become as accessible to them as He was to Adam before the Fall, just as He had been foreshadowed by the rock in Moses' time.

On this mountain, however, as the curtain between heaven and earth was momentarily peeled back, the glory began to shine forth as in the former days. So, once again, the cloud descended to protect fallen man.

> . . . *and behold a voice out of the cloud, which said, This is my beloved Son, in whom I am well pleased; hear ye him.*
>
> *And when the disciples heard it, they fell on their face, and were sore afraid.*
>
> Matthew 17:5,6

For a few moments, a window between heaven and earth had been opened. Through that window came a message from the throne of God, and it still applies to us today: "This is my beloved Son . . . hear ye him."

## The Glory Today

Earthly manifestations of God's glory did not end that day on the mountain. A few months later, following Jesus' death, resurrection, and ascension to heaven, an event occurred that was unprecedented in the history of the world. It was an event that would make the glory, presence, and power of God available to you and me. We read about it in Acts, chapter 2:

> And when the day of Pentecost was fully come, they were all with one accord in one place.
>
> And suddenly there came a sound from heaven as of a rushing mighty wind, and it filled all the house where they were sitting.
>
> And there appeared unto them cloven tongues like as of fire, and it sat upon each of them.
>
> And they were all filled with the Holy Ghost, and began to speak with other tongues, as the Spirit gave them utterance.
>
> Acts 2:1–4

On this remarkable day, the Spirit of Almighty God was poured out upon man. To that point, the Holy Ghost had only rested upon man for short periods of time. Now the Spirit was available to abide within man, indwelling them twenty-four hours a day and supercharging them with the power of God.

Moments after the event just described had occurred, the apostle Peter preached a Holy Ghost-inspired sermon to explain what had taken place:

*But Peter, standing up with the eleven, lifted up his voice, and said unto them, Ye men of Judaea, and all ye that dwell at Jerusalem, be this known unto you, and hearken to my words:*

*For these are not drunken, as ye suppose, seeing it is but the third hour of the day.*

*But this is that which was spoken by the prophet Joel;*

*And it shall come to pass in the last days, saith God, I will pour out of my Spirit upon all flesh: and your sons and your daughters shall prophesy, and your young men shall see visions, and your old men shall dream dreams:*

*And they were all filled with the Holy Ghost, and began to speak with other tongues, as the Spirit gave them utterance.*

Acts 2:14–18

Pentecost brought a whole new dimension to experiencing the presence of God. In fact, it almost brings us full circle to where Adam was before the Fall. Adam had the life of God inside himself; so too can we, as believers, have the life of God inside us.

God's brilliant master plan for restoring man to fellowship with Himself is nearly complete. It brings us, however, to these questions: Why did God pursue man's fellowship so forcefully? What moved Him to put a garden in the east of Eden in the first place?

The answers to these questions are tied up in a concept called the *mercy of God*. Let's consider this topic next.

## Claim Your Benefits!

And it shall come to pass in the last days, saith God, I will pour out of my Spirit upon all flesh: and your sons and your daughters shall prophesy, and your young men shall see visions, and your old men shall dream dreams.

Acts 2:17

## My prayer in the power of the Word . . .

_____

_____

_____

_____

_____

_____

## Study Questions

1. How was God's presence manifested to Moses?

_____

_____

_____

_____

_____

2. How would you describe the relationship Moses had with the Lord?

_____

_____

_____

_____

3. How is God's glory manifested today?

_____

_____

_____

_____

_____

4. What sort of relationship would you like to have with the Lord?

_____

_____

_____

_____

_____

4

# The Mercies of God

For thousands of years, many people have been trying to figure out God. They want to know what makes Him do what He does. For the most part, such people have been 100 percent wrong.

The reason so many fail to discern the heart of God is because it is impossible to do so apart from an understanding of the mercies of God.

God's mercy permeates and motivates everything He has ever done. If you are trying to comprehend God with the presupposition that He is nothing but a harsh God of wrath and vengeance, you will never see an accurate picture.

## The Checed of God

Throughout the Old Testament you will find a word which, in the original Hebrew language, is *checed*.[1] It is often translated mercy, *kindness*, *lovingkindness*, or *goodness*. This word, *checed*, is almost always in reference to God's feelings or actions toward man by displaying His mercy, kindness, favor, and goodness.

Based on *Strong's Exhaustive Concordance*, the word *checed* is translated in the following ways, indicating the number of times each word is used:

1. kindness—40

2. mercy—15

3. lovingkindness—30

4. goodness—10

5. goodliness—1

6. good—1

7. favor—3

This totals 100 times that *checed* is used when being translated as only these seven words.

In the New Testament there is a similar term in Greek, *agape*. This term is used 139 times and is usually translated *love*. We see it in John 3:16, which says, "For God so *loved* the world, that he gave. . . ."

Both *checed* and *agape* represent the God-kind of love, the kind of love that gives sacrificially and unselfishly; in other words, mercy.

If you want to understand God, His nature, and His ways, you must gain an understanding of His mercies.

## God Is Good

The religious, guilt-ridden mind-set likes to see God as a mean, spiteful dictator, who is ready to thump you on the head the moment you get out of line. Many with such a mind-set also believe He likes to put sickness or tragedy in your life to test you or teach you a lesson.

This, however, is not the God of the Bible. A careful search of the Scriptures will reveal a much different sort of God. Look, for example, at Psalm 136:

> O give thanks unto the Lord; for he is good: for his mercy endureth for ever.
>
> O give thanks unto the God of gods: for his mercy endureth for ever.
>
> O give thanks to the Lord of lords: for his mercy endureth for ever.
>
> To him who alone doeth great wonders: for his mercy endureth for ever.
>
> To him that by wisdom made the heavens: for his mercy endureth for ever.

To him that stretched out the earth above the waters: for his mercy endureth for ever.

To him that made great lights: for his mercy endureth for ever:

The sun to rule by day: for his mercy endureth for ever:

The moon and stars to rule by night: for his mercy endureth for ever.

To him that smote Egypt in their firstborn: for his mercy endureth for ever:

And brought out Israel from among them: for his mercy endureth for ever:

With a strong hand, and with a stretched out arm: for his mercy endureth for ever.

To him which divided the Red sea into parts: for his mercy endureth for ever:

And made Israel to pass through the midst of it: for his mercy endureth for ever:

But overthrew Pharaoh and his host in the Red sea: for his mercy endureth for ever.

To him which led his people through the wilderness: for his mercy endureth for ever.

To him which smote great kings: for his mercy endureth for ever:

And slew famous kings: for his mercy endureth for ever:

*Sihon king of the Amorites: for his mercy endureth for ever:*

*And Og the king of Bashan: for his mercy endureth for ever:*

*And gave their land for an heritage: for his mercy endureth for ever:*

*Even an heritage unto Israel his servant: for his mercy endureth for ever.*

*Who remembered us in our low estate: for his mercy endureth for ever:*

*And hath redeemed us from our enemies: for his mercy endureth for ever.*

*Who giveth food to all flesh: for his mercy endureth for ever.*

*O give thanks unto the God of heaven: for his mercy endureth for ever.*

Do you get the picture? I believe God wants us to know this twofold truth: He is good and His mercy endures forever!

God is motivated by love and mercy. It is a theme found from the books of Genesis to Revelation. In fact, the Bible is nothing more than a love story—the story of God's love and pursuit of fallen man.

Let's read from 1 Chronicles, chapter 16:

*For great is the Lord, and greatly to be praised: he also is to be feared above all gods.*

*For all the gods of the people are idols: but the Lord made the heavens.*

*Glory and honour are in his presence; strength and gladness are in his place.*

*Give unto the Lord, ye kindreds of the people, give unto the Lord glory and strength.*

*Give unto the Lord the glory due unto his name: bring an offering, and come before him: worship the Lord in the beauty of holiness.*

*Fear before him, all the earth: the world also shall be stable, that it be not moved.*

*Let the heavens be glad, and let the earth rejoice: and let men say among the nations, The Lord reigneth.*

*Let the sea roar, and the fulness thereof: let the fields rejoice, and all that is therein.*

*Then shall the trees of the wood sing out at the presence of the Lord, because he cometh to judge the earth.*

**O give thanks unto the Lord; for he is good; for his mercy endureth for ever.**

1 Chronicles 16:25–34

Sound familiar? We need to get this truth: *God is good and His mercy lasts forever!*

Far too many believers are still walking around in constant fear that God is going to "get them." Is that how you feel?

Think about it this way: If God were going to "get you" because you mess up every now and then, you would have been "got" a long time ago!

God is good. He radiates goodness. Do you remember the words God used with Moses on the mountain when he asked God to remove the cloud and to reveal Himself? When Moses said to Him, "Show me Your glory!" God answered, "I will make all my goodness pass before thee . . ." (Ex. 33:19).

As far as God is concerned, when we are looking at Him, we are seeing His goodness. God and His goodness are inseparable; they are one and the same.

## A Battle Cry of Mercy!

Mercy is the cornerstone and centerpiece of everything God has ever done in the earth. When God's people remind themselves of that mercy, it opens the door to all of heaven's power and resources. That is just what we see happening in 2 Chronicles 20.

God's people, led by King Jehoshaphat, were surrounded by powerful, hostile forces. They were greatly outnumbered and out-armed. To the natural eye, they surely seemed to be doomed.

In a time of fasting and prayer, God gave Jehoshaphat some instructions. God said, ". . . the battle is not yours, but God's. . . . To morrow go ye down against them. . . . Ye shall not need to fight in this battle: set yourselves, stand ye still, and see the salvation of the Lord with you, O Judah and Jerusalem: fear not, nor be dismayed; tomorrow go out against them: for the Lord will be with you" (2 Chron. 20:15–17).

Once they heard this, Jehoshaphat and the Israelites began worshipping and praising God. The next morning Jehoshaphat consulted with the people then sent out praisers before the army. They faced the enemy in battle, being led not by their strongest troops but by the praise singers!

> And when he had consulted with the people, he appointed singers unto the Lord, and that should praise the beauty of holiness, as they went out before the army, and to say, **Praise the Lord; for his mercy endureth for ever.**
>
> 2 Chronicles 20:21

When you are faced with a life-and-death crisis, the most important thing you can remind yourself is that God's mercy endures forever. It will stir your faith. It will move you to tap in to the power of praise. It will bring God onto the scene to show Himself strong on your behalf.

That's precisely what happened in the case of Jehoshaphat.

> And when they began to sing and to praise, the Lord set ambushments against the children of Ammon,

41

*Moab, and mount Seir, which were come against Judah; and they were smitten.*

2 Chronicles 20:22

When you have the mercy of God directed at you, no power in hell can stand against you. When those praisers started singing out the mercy of God, they were, in effect, declaring to their enemy: "We are God's beloved, so you will leave us alone if you know what's good for you! Touch not the anointed of God!"

God's mercy will put your enemies to flight!

When the enemy of cancer seems to have surrounded you, God's mercy will cause Him to say to you, "I am the Lord that healeth thee" (Ex. 15:26).

When financial lack tries to keep you in poverty, God's mercy speaks through Him, saying to you: "I will bless thee coming in, and I will bless thee going out. I will supply all your needs according to My riches in glory!" (Deut. 28:6; Phil. 4:19.)

When rebellion tries to come against your children, the mercy of God says to you: "All thy children shall be taught of the Lord; and great shall be the peace of thy children" (Isa. 54:13).

Understanding and remembering God's mercy is a matter of life and death. A wrong conception of God is causing Christians to be killed every day.

## Mercy and "the Presence"

An awareness of God's mercy is closely tied to His presence. If you want to experience the benefits of God's presence, you need to understand the depths of His mercy.

Reminding yourself of God's mercy and praising Him for it will bring His presence on the scene in a powerful way. This is what we see happening with King Solomon and the people of God in 2 Chronicles, chapter 5.

Solomon and the people were dedicating the new temple and celebrating the arrival of the ark of the covenant. The ark of the covenant symbolized God's presence among His people. Look what happened when they began to sing of His goodness and mercy:

> It came even to pass, as the trumpeters and singers were as one, to make one sound to be heard in praising and thanking the Lord; and when they lifted up their voice with the trumpets and cymbals and instruments of musick, and praised the Lord, saying, **For he is good; for his mercy endureth for ever:** that then the house was filled with a cloud, even the house of the Lord;
>
> So that the priests could not stand to minister by reason of the cloud: for the glory of the Lord had filled the house of God.
>
> 2 Chronicles 5:13,14

Do you see how God's mercy is linked to His presence? When Israel began to sing of God's goodness and mercy, God's presence became so strong in that place that the priests couldn't stand up under it!

Few things will bring God's presence onto the scene faster in your life than to remind yourself of God's mercy and to start wholeheartedly praising Him for it. You can stand on the mercy of God.

## Sweat Won't Get It

Now that you know what brings God's power and presence into your situation, you need to know what won't bring it in: namely, all your hard work.

Traditional religion has taught a lot of believers about doing good works for God. If only they can do enough good works or spend enough hours reading their Bible, somehow they will have earned enough Brownie points with God to get Him to do something for them.

Even as a child of God, nothing you could do can make God love you any more than He already does. His *checed* for you is complete and everlasting. In fact, it's an insult to God's mercy for you to think that any religious work you could possibly do would be enough to pay for what He has freely given you.

Good works are great. Fasting is beneficial. Reading the Word of God is essential to spiritual growth. But when you fall into the trap of thinking those things will *earn* you more favor with God, you have moved out of faith and into cold, dead religion.

God loves you. It's that simple. It's His mercy that brings Him into your toughest situations to save you from the consequences.

Sweat doesn't bring in the presence of God. His presence comes as a result of His mercy.

## Mercy Has It Covered

If you have not yet figured out that mercy plays a big role in everything God does, some words from Psalm 145 should remove all doubt:

> The Lord is gracious, and full of compassion; slow to anger, and of great mercy.
> The Lord is good to all: and **his tender mercies are over all his works.**

> Psalm 145:8,9

God's mercy is "over *all* his works"! Everything He does is based on mercy. When He heals you, it is because of His mercy. When He gives you the finances to pay a bill, it is because of mercy. Even your salvation—the act of being born again—is based on mercy. The apostle Paul said it this way:

45

*For by grace are ye saved through faith; and that not of*
*yourselves: it is the gift of God:*
   *Not of works, lest any man should boast.*

Ephesians 2:8,9

Don't fall into the trap of thinking that just because you messed up and sinned you are disqualified from God's favor and mercy. On the contrary, you are a candidate for it! God's mercy is over all His works; and, as His child, you are one of His works.

God's mercy will outlast your sin. If you fall, God's mercy will still be there. His love will be there. His kindness will be there.

Is that a license for you to sin? No way!

Get a revelation of this truth, and you will not want to sin. You will start hating the presence of sin in your life as much as God does.

Proverbs 16:6 says, "By mercy and truth iniquity is purged. . . ." Mercy does not invite the presence of sin into your life; it drives it out!

## *Look Behind You*

Many believers are under the impression that trouble is following them. They are talking about it all the time, saying things like, "It just seems that everything I do turns out no good," or "I never get a break; trouble just seems to follow me wherever I go." They may think this way, but it's a lie from the pit of hell!

The truth is, if you are a child of God, it is His mercy—not trouble—that is following you. Psalm 23:6 says so:

> Surely **goodness and mercy shall follow me** all the days of my life: and I will dwell in the house of the Lord for ever.

The Hebrew word *râdaph*,[2] translated "follow" in this verse, means "to follow (after, on), hunt, (be under) . . . pursue."

As a believer, God's goodness and mercy is in hot pursuit of you wherever you go. You can't outrun it. You can't give it the slip. You can't move out of its range.

*Checed* and *agape*—in other words, God's goodness and mercy—are the agents that bring God's presence into your life and into your every situation. You can't understand God's presence without a solid understanding of His mercy. Let's look further into this subject of His mercy.

## Claim Your Benefits!

O give thanks unto the Lord; for he is good: for his mercy endureth for ever.
O give thanks unto the God of gods: for his mercy endureth for ever.
O give thanks to the Lord of lords: for his mercy endureth for ever.

Psalm 136:1–3

## My prayer in the power of the Word . . .

_____

_____

_____

_____

_____

_____

_____

## Study Questions

1. What do we mean when we say "the mercy of God"?

_____

_____

_____

_____

_____

2. Why is mercy so important to our relationship with God?

_____

_____

_____

_____

_____

3. How have you experienced His mercy?

_____

_____

_____

_____

_____

4. How does Ephesians 2:8,9 demonstrate God's mercy?

_____

_____

_____

_____

_____

# 5

# *Developing Faith for the Mercies of God*

A T THIS POINT I can almost hear you thinking, *If God's mercy is following me and His mercy brings all the benefits of God's presence into my life, why am I not experiencing all those benefits?*

There is a simple answer to your question. It is not enough to have God's mercy directed towards you. Like everything else in the Christian life, your faith activates that mercy to bring it into manifestation.

The Bible is full of promises for believers—promises of healing, abundance, peace, safety, and so much more. Yet most believers never see those promises become a reality in their lives because they never develop faith for those promises. *Faith is the key.*

Ephesians 2:8 tells us it is by faith that we are saved:

> *For by grace are ye saved through faith; and that not of yourselves: it is the gift of God.*

According to Colossians 2:6–7, we must live the Christian life the same way we got saved:

> *As ye have therefore received Christ Jesus the Lord, so walk ye in him:*
> *Rooted and built up in him, and stablished in the faith, as ye have been taught. . . .*

In other words, you successfully live the Christian life the same way you started it—by faith. Romans 1:17 echoes this truth:

> *For therein is the righteousness of God revealed from faith to faith: as it is written,* **The just shall live by faith.**

Now you can begin to see why so few Christians experience the benefits of God's abundant mercies. They have no faith either to receive these benefits or to live in them. On the contrary, they have faith in the idea that God is mad at them, that He's "out to get them," that He's just looking for an opportunity to zap them. Is it any wonder then that so few believers can really understand the mercies of God?

The good news is, you can make a change in your life starting right now. How? According to Romans 10:17, by hearing the Word!

> *So then faith cometh by hearing, and hearing by the word of God.*

## The Word of Mercy

In the previous chapter, we got a small sampling of what the Word has to say regarding God's mercy. We saw Scripture after Scripture declaring how God's "mercy endureth for ever." In fact, this phrase is repeated forty-two times in the Old Testament alone!

We also discovered that God's mercy is over all His works. (Ps. 145:9.) God's mercy is literally in hot pursuit of you. (Ps. 23:6.)

You need to meditate on these Scriptures and get these truths planted deeply into your spirit. As you hear the Word concerning God's mercy, faith in that mercy will come. Then and only then will you begin to see the full manifestation of His mercy in your life.

Let me warn you, though. Your natural mind will not want to accept the reality of God's mercy. Both your mind and the devil will be telling you how unworthy you are for God to be doing anything good in your life. Unless you get a firm, unshakable revelation of God's mercy, the devil will always be able to rob you of your confidence before God.

Without an understanding of mercy, every time you try to step out and do anything of spiritual value, the enemy will bring up every mistake you have ever made. That's why it is so vital that you get this truth firmly established in your heart and mind. Once you do, the devil doesn't stand a chance.

For example, when you prepare to go into the presence of God and receive His promises, the devil will try to shake your confidence, reminding you of some sin you have committed. But if you are grounded in God's mercy, you can just cut the devil to shreds with God's Word.

You can say to him: "No, devil, you're a liar! I'm a child of God and His mercy is over all His works. His mercy endureth forever. I've confessed that sin and put it under the blood of Jesus. God's Word says that if I confess my sins, He is faithful and just to forgive my sins and cleanse me from all unrighteousness." (1 John 1:9.)

Don't go around declaring your unworthiness to receive the presence and promises of God. Instead, say you *are* worthy because God has declared you so. You have been made the righteousness of God in Christ Jesus and have been seated with Him in heavenly places. (2 Cor. 5:21; Eph. 2:6.)

You must realize that God doesn't see you the way you see yourself. If you are born again, God sees you through the blood of His Son, Jesus. He is not looking at you alone; He sees you in Christ.

To get a powerful picture of this, go to the first chapter of Ephesians and note every instance of such phrases as *in Christ, in Him,* or *in the Beloved.* You will find the following descriptions about being *in Christ:*

- You are blessed with all spiritual blessings in heavenly places. (v. 3.)

- You are chosen before the foundation of the world, that you should be holy and without blame before Him. (v. 4.)

- You are predestinated unto the adoption of children. (v. 5.)

- You are accepted. (v. 6.)

- You have redemption through His blood, the forgiveness of sins, according to the riches of His grace. (v. 7.)

- You have obtained an inheritance. (v. 11.)

- You are sealed with the Holy Spirit of promise. (v. 13.)

- You have been given the spirit of wisdom and revelation in the knowledge of Him. (v. 17.)

Are you beginning to get the idea that being in Christ changes your standing with God a little bit?

Quit calling yourself unworthy. It's an insult to the grace and mercy of God.

## *Mercy Meditation*

Reading and hearing the Word concerning God's mercy is vital. But to develop faith in the mercies of God, you need to take another step and begin to meditate on the Word.

Psalm 1 says that a man who meditates day and night on the Word is ". . . like a tree planted by the rivers of water, that bringeth forth his fruit in his season; his leaf also shall not wither; and whatsoever he doeth shall prosper" (v. 3).

Meditating on God's Word does not mean sitting cross-legged on the floor, humming and chanting for twelve hours a day. Bible meditations simply means dwelling on or pondering a portion of God's Word. You can be doing this while you are taking a shower, driving your car, cooking a meal, or even drifting off to sleep at night.

As you are mulling over God's Word throughout the day, something powerful will start happening in your spirit. That Word will begin to take root and bear fruit—the fruit of faith.

The psalmist David knew a little bit about the *checed*, or the mercy of God. Many of the psalms focus on it. These psalms make ideal Scriptures on which to meditate. Let's look, for example, at certain verses from the book of Psalms:

*All the paths of the Lord are mercy and truth unto such as keep his covenant and his testimonies.*

Psalm 25:10

*I will be glad and rejoice in thy mercy: for thou hast considered my trouble; thou hast known my soul in adversities.*

Psalm 31:7

*For thou, Lord, art good, and ready to forgive; and plenteous in mercy unto all them that call upon thee.*

Psalm 86:5

*The Lord is merciful and gracious, slow to anger, and plenteous in mercy.*

*For as the heaven is high above the earth, so great is his mercy toward them that fear him.*

*But the mercy of the Lord is from everlasting to everlasting upon them that fear him. . . .*

Psalm 103:8,11,17

As a child of God, your heavenly Father has an inexhaustible supply of mercy toward you. You can't wear it out and you can't outrun it. Once you get this truth into your heart—developing faith in it—you will never shrink from God's presence again.

Faith in the mercies of God will equip you to enjoy the benefits of His presence like nothing else can.

## *The Power of Compassion*

The Bible uses another term which is linked to the *checed* and *agape* of God. This word is *compassion*.

The first part of Psalm 145:8, a verse we have already examined, makes clear the relationship between compassion and mercy:

> *The Lord is gracious, and **full of compassion;** slow to anger, and of great mercy.*

As you know, Jesus was a perfect representation of the heart and nature of God. Jesus said, ". . . he that hath seen me hath seen the Father" (John 14:9). You don't have to look for long at the life of Jesus to discover He was a man of compassion.

Here is a sampling of verses showing Jesus being moved with compassion:

> *But when he [Jesus] saw the multitudes, he was moved with compassion on them, because they fainted, and were scattered abroad, as sheep having no shepherd.*
>
> Matthew 9:36

*And Jesus went forth, and saw a great multitude, and was moved with compassion toward them, and he healed their sick.*

Matthew 14:14

*Then Jesus called his disciples unto him, and said, I have compassion on the multitude, because they continue with me now three days, and have nothing to eat: and I will not send them away fasting, lest they faint in the way.*

Matthew 15:32

*So Jesus had compassion on them, and touched their eyes: and immediately their eyes received sight, and they followed him.*

Matthew 20:34

*And Jesus, moved with compassion, put forth his hand, and touched him, and saith unto him, I will; be thou clean.*

Mark 1:41

*And when the Lord saw her, he had compassion on her, and said unto her, Weep not.*

Luke 7:13

Over and over again in Scripture, we see how Jesus' compassion moved Him to meet the needs of the people. If you want to understand the heart of Jesus, you must start with an understanding of His compassion. He described His mission as one of coming "to seek and to save that which was lost" (Luke 19:10).

What does all this have to do with the presence of God? Everything!

Understanding the compassion which God has toward you will totally change your attitude about spending time in His presence. As we have seen, it is only in His presence that you can enjoy the benefits of healing, prosperity, peace, and power.

## Claim Your Benefits!

For by grace are ye saved through faith; and that not of yourselves: it is the gift of God.

Ephesians 2:8

### My prayer in the power of the Word . . .

_____

_____

_____

_____

_____

_____

_____

## Study Questions

1. How does one's faith activate God's mercy?

_____

_____

_____

_____

_____

2. Why do you suppose so few people experience the benefit of God's abundant mercy?

_____

_____

_____

_____

3. What does the Bible mean when it tells us God's mercy "endures forever"?

_____

_____

_____

_____

_____

4. How does experiencing God's mercy lead us to care for others?

_____

_____

_____

_____

_____

6

# The Ministry of Comfort

As we have seen in the previous chapters, both God the Father and God the Son (Jesus) are motivated by a strong heart of mercy, lovingkindness, and compassion.

This mercy drives and motivates all that God has ever done in history, and it dominates the way He responds to us today. As we have observed several times in the Word of God:

> *The Lord is gracious, and full of compassion; slow to anger, and of great mercy.*
> *The Lord is good to all: and his tender mercies are over all his works.*

Psalm 145:8,9

There is still another word in the Bible that describes an aspect of the mercies of God: *comfort.*

## *"The God of All Comfort"*

In 2 Corinthians 1:3, God is called "the God of *all* comfort":

> *Blessed be God, even the Father of our Lord Jesus Christ, the Father of mercies, and the God of all comfort.*

Likewise, Jesus referred to the Holy Spirit as "another Comforter" (John 14:16).

All of these add up to one truth: Comfort is a major attribute of all three members of the Godhead—Father, Son, and Holy Ghost. If the Spirit of God dwells within you, a believer, then the same should be true of you!

As believers in Jesus Christ, we should have a ministry of mercy and comfort. In fact, that is the very truth we find in 2 Corinthians 1:3. Let's take a look at this verse again and continue on with verse 4:

> *Blessed be God, even the Father of our Lord Jesus Christ, the Father of mercies, and the God of all comfort;*
>
> *Who comforteth us in all our tribulation, that we may be able to comfort them which are in any trouble, by the comfort wherewith we ourselves are comforted of God.*
>
> 2 Corinthians 1:3,4

If you are a believer, then you have a ministry of comfort. But according to the verses we just read, you can't *give* comfort unless you have *received* it.

How do you receive comfort? By getting into the presence of "the God of *all* comfort"!

As we continue to explore the Word, we will see that comfort and compassion are two sides of the same coin.

## Set Free by Compassion

In the fifth chapter of Mark's gospel, we find the remarkable account of Jesus' encounter with the madman of Gadara. We see here a man so bound up by Satan that deliverance seemed unthinkable.

> And they came over unto the other side of the sea, into the country of the Gadarenes.
>
> And when he [Jesus] was come out of the ship, immediately there met him out of the tombs a man with an unclean spirit,
>
> Who had his dwelling among the tombs; and no man could bind him, no, not with chains:
>
> Because that he had been often bound with fetters and chains, and the chains had been plucked asunder by him, and the fetters broken in pieces: neither could any man tame him.

*And always, night and day, he was in the mountains, and in the tombs, crying, and cutting himself with stones.*

Mark 5:1–5

This man was such a prisoner of Satan that even his physical body was energized by demonic power.

Maybe you, a child of God, are bound up in some way today. No matter what might have you bound—whether it be some form of addiction, habit, or lifestyle—you are no more a slave to it than this man of Gadara was.

Look at Jesus' response to this situation:

*But when he saw Jesus afar off, he ran and worshipped him,*

*And cried with a loud voice, and said, What have I to do with thee, Jesus, thou Son of the most high God? I adjure thee by God, that thou torment me not.*

*For he said unto him, Come out of the man, thou unclean spirit.*

Mark 5:6–8

Did Jesus reject the man or tell him he had to go away and clean up his act first before he could be ministered to? No. Jesus immediately set about to address this man's need.

*Now there was there nigh unto the mountains a great herd of swine feeding.*

*And all the devils besought him, saying, Send us into the swine, that we may enter into them.*

*And forthwith Jesus gave them leave. And the unclean spirits went out, and entered into the swine: and the herd ran violently down a steep place into the sea, (they were about two thousand;) and were choked in the sea.*

Mark 5:11–13

Once the man had been delivered from bondage, he asked if he could join Jesus' disciples. Instead, Jesus gave him a mission:

*Howbeit Jesus suffered him not, but saith unto him, Go home to thy friends, and tell them how great things the Lord hath done for thee, **and hath had compassion on thee.***

*And he departed, and began to publish in Decapolis how great things Jesus had done for him: and all men did marvel.*

Mark 5:19,20

Do you see Jesus' motivation for ministering this man's deliverance? It was compassion. Jesus sent him back to his hometown with a message concerning the compassion of God.

68

This is a message we as recipients of the mercies of God should be offering to the world every day. Far too many of us are doing the opposite. By our negative words and defeated lifestyles, we are carrying a message that God is mean, neglectful, and stingy.

Of course, we know God is none of these things. But we are sending out this message to those around us when we are not delivering a victorious, faith-filled message of God's goodness and mercy.

## *"Have Mercy on Us!"*

Another classic example of Jesus' compassion in action is found in Matthew, chapter 20. In verse 29 we find Jesus on His way out of Jericho, accompanied by a large following of people:

> *And, behold, two blind men sitting by the way side, when they heard that Jesus passed by, cried out, saying, Have mercy on us, O Lord, thou Son of David.*
>
> *And the multitude rebuked them, because they should hold their peace: but they cried the more, saying, Have mercy on us, O Lord, thou Son of David.*
>
> Matthew 20:30,31

These two men made one of the most effective appeals to God—an appeal to His mercy. How did Jesus respond?

*And Jesus stood still, and called them, and said, What will ye that I shall do unto you?*

Matthew 20:32

This is a good reminder that you should always be specific in your prayers and petitions. Don't just pray, "Bless me, Lord." Be specific.

Jesus wanted to know precisely what these men were believing God for.

> *They say unto him, Lord, that our eyes may be opened.*

Matthew 20:33

Here is how Jesus responded to their request:

> **So Jesus had compassion on them,** *and touched their eyes: and immediately their eyes received sight, and they followed him.*

Matthew 20:34

We can see the wonderful thing about the kind of compassion Jesus has for us. Not only is He moved emotionally by our circumstances, He is also moved to do something about them! Just having someone to feel sorry for you does you no good whatsoever. Help comes by getting your need met. That's the kind of compassion Jesus has for you.

## Compassion Removes Doubt

I hope by now you are noticing that the entire Bible is, first and foremost, a revelation of the mercy, love, and grace of God. We see another aspect of this revelation in Mark, chapter 1:

> And there came a leper to him, beseeching him, and kneeling down to him, and saying unto him, If thou wilt, thou canst make me clean.
>
> And Jesus, **moved with compassion,** put forth his hand, and touched him, and saith unto him, I will; be thou clean.
>
> And as soon as he had spoken, immediately the leprosy departed from him, and he was cleansed.

Mark 1:40–42

Notice what this man was saying to Jesus: "I know You can heal me; I'm just not sure You *will.*"

It was excusable for him to be unsure about the will of God because he had no knowledge of God's Word. But for us today as believers to feel this way would be an insult to our heavenly Father. His will to heal has been made abundantly clear in His Word.

Of course, Jesus' response to this man was consistent with everything else we have seen thus far. Notice again verse 41:

*And Jesus, moved with compassion, put forth his hand, and touched him, and saith unto him, I will; be thou clean.*

We see here a sequence in Jesus' activities.

First, Jesus was "moved with compassion."

Second, this compassion moved Him to reach out to the man. "Jesus . . . put forth his hand, and touched him."

Third, Jesus addressed the man's doubts about God's will to heal. "Jesus . . . saith unto him, I will; be thou clean." You see, Jesus had to deal with that doubt before the man could receive his healing. Jesus had to make sure the man knew God wanted him healed.

The same is true for us today. We need to go to the Word and get our doubts removed before we will be able to receive the promises of God. Far too many believers are still in the place of thinking, *I know God **can**; I'm just not sure He **will**.*

Millions of Christians have been told that God would put cancer on them to teach them a spiritual lesson or to build their character. They have been told God would take the life of one of their children in order to accomplish His purposes in the earth.

These are lies—lies against the character and compassion

of God. God does not need sickness and tragedy to teach you anything. He has His Word and His Holy Spirit to teach you whatever you need to know.

You must get this issue settled in your mind before you will be able to receive. Nothing can help you do this more effectively than an understanding that Jesus' response to your need will always be one of compassion.

## Claim Your Benefits!

Blessed be God, even the Father of our Lord Jesus Christ, the Father of mercies, and the God of all comfort.

2 Corinthians 1:3

## My prayer in the power of the Word . . .

_____

_____

_____

_____

_____

_____

_____

## Study Questions

1. In what way is comfort an important aspect of God's character?

_____

_____

_____

_____

_____

2. Whom do you know who demonstrates compassion?

_____

_____

_____

_____

_____

3. When have you been able to demonstrate compassion to others?

_____

_____

_____

_____

4. In what way does compassion remove doubt?

_____

_____

_____

_____

_____

# The Operation of Mercy in the Believer's Life

I T  I S  O N E thing for you to know God is merciful. It is another thing for you to have an understanding of *how* that mercy will operate in your life on a practical, day-to-day basis. That is the focus of this chapter.

In Ephesians, chapter 2, we find a fascinating portion of Scripture that sheds some light on this issue. The first few verses paint a dark picture of where we all were before Jesus saved us.

> *And you were dead in your trespasses and sins, in which you formerly walked according to the course of this world, according to the prince of the power of the air, of the spirit that is now working in the sons of disobedience.*

*Among them we too all formerly lived in the lusts of our flesh, indulging the desires of the flesh and of the mind, and were by nature children of wrath, even as the rest.*

Ephesians 2:1–3 NAS

Then the apostle Paul brings us the glorious news of how and why we are no longer in that horrible state:

*But God, being rich in mercy, because of His great love with which He loved us, even when we were dead in our transgressions, made us alive together with Christ (by grace you have been saved).*

Ephesians 2:4,5 NAS

Why did God make us alive together with Christ? Because He is rich in mercy. In fact, the entire grand plan of salvation is a direct result of the love and mercy of God.

The love of God produced the Virgin Birth. God's love produced the plan for man's redemption from sin. God's love produced the baptism of the Holy Spirit. The love of God gave us our access to Him through prayer.

Everything we have a right to as believers (and that's more than you can imagine) is a direct product of the love and mercy of God. These things did not spring from a mind that was set on vengeance. They did not come from a God who takes pleasure in destruction.

All of this, of course, is contrary to popular religious opinion.

## You Be the Judge

At this point you may be asking yourself, *Isn't God a Judge who rewards or punishes based on our actions?*

The answer to this question is twofold: yes and no. The truth is, God does not want to be put in the place of judging our lives; He wants us to do that. Look at 1 Corinthians 11:31:

> For if we would judge ourselves, we should not be judged.

This verse means it is God's best for each believer to judge himself. If you will be vigilant about comparing your behavior to the standard of the Word, you will never have a need for God or anyone else to judge you.

Of course, the flip side of that coin is this: If you refuse to judge yourself, you will be judged by an external source. Failure to judge yourself will hinder God's ability to bless you as He wants.

When you refuse to examine your life and eliminate those things that don't please God, you put God in the position of having to point out those things to you. The good news is, God judges in mercy. As far as believers are concerned, the judgment of God is always a judgment motivated by love and designed to bring about restoration, healing, and blessing.

## *Conviction vs. Condemnation*

Often, a believer who has sinned will mistake conviction for condemnation. When you blow it, two things usually happen: The Spirit of God moves in to *convict* you of that sin, and the devil moves in to *condemn* you for it.

The *conviction* of God is designed to bring you back into fellowship with Him through repentance and forgiveness. The *condemnation* of the devil is designed to shame you into pulling away from God. Satan wants to drive a wedge between you and your Source of life.

The next time you sin, respond to conviction and reject condemnation. The Word says, "If we confess our sins, he is faithful and just to forgive us our sins, and to cleanse us from all unrighteousness" (1 John 1:9).

When the enemy starts whispering condemnation in your ear, hit him with Romans 8:1:

> *There is therefore now **no condemnation** to them which are in Christ Jesus, who walk not after the flesh, but after the Spirit.*

If you have allowed condemnation to drive a wedge between you and God, you can take care of it right now. Just lift your hands and say this prayer:

> *In the name of Jesus, by faith I receive forgiveness. I forgive myself as I forgive others. I will no longer be condemned by the acts of my past. They have been taken care of by God Almighty and I have been judged by the mercy of God. God has judged me as being righteous. I am what He has judged me to be: right with Him! I receive restoration of my fellowship with God right now, in the name of Jesus.*

From this moment on, you should always respond to the conviction of the Holy Spirit and never to the condemning voice of the enemy. How will you know the difference? The first—conviction—will always draw you to God. The second—condemnation—will always make you want to hide from God's presence.

Whenever you blow it, immediately run to God. He will meet you with the open arms of mercy. *"His mercy endureth for ever."*

## Taking Hold of the Mercy of God

Is there anyone among us today who doesn't desperately need the mercy of God? The truth is, we all need it. Without the mercy of God we would all be lost. Every moment of every day, you and I need to be able to access the provision and power that come from the mercy of God.

The question is, How do we lay hold of the mercy that we all need?

The answer can be found in Hebrews, chapter 4. Here we find a description of Jesus as our High Priest, representing us before God.

> *For we have not an high priest which cannot be touched with the feeling of our infirmities; but was in all points tempted like as we are, yet without sin.*
>
> *Let us therefore* **come boldly unto the throne of grace, that we may obtain mercy,** *and find grace to help in time of need.*
>
> Hebrews 4:15,16

This is the key to getting all of the mercy, grace, and help that we need: simply *"come boldly."*

You and I have a High Priest in heaven who knows what it feels like to be clothed in the weakness of human flesh. He experienced every temptation we have ever fallen into, yet He never sinned.

As a result, we are commanded to come to God's throne for help and to do it *boldly*.

This does not say you are to slink into God's throne room on your belly, groveling at the feet of God and muttering how unworthy you are. It does not say you have to come to God with your head down and your tail between your legs.

Instead, you are to come boldly. Why? Because Jesus is your High Priest. It is His blood that was sprinkled on the mercy seat to cleanse you of all unrighteousness. He is your representative in heaven; therefore, you are just as welcome in the throne room of God as He is. Hallelujah!

The mercy of God is yours. Come and get it!

## Claim Your Benefits!

But God, being rich in mercy, because of His great love with which He loved us, even when we were dead in our transgressions, made us alive together with Christ (by grace you have been saved).

Ephesians 2:4,5 NAS

## My prayer in the power of the Word . . .

_____

_____

_____

_____

_____

_____

_____

## Study Questions

1. What does Ephesians 2:15 teach us about compassion and mercy?

_____

_____

_____

_____

_____

2. If a friend said to you, "God judges us solely on the basis of our actions," how would you respond?

_____

_____

_____

_____

_____

3. What is the difference between *conviction* and *condemnation*?

_____

_____

_____

_____

_____

4. In your own words, how can someone take hold of the mercy of God?

_____

_____

_____

_____

_____

# Living in the Presence of God

IN THE CHURCH where I pastor, there are many different rooms with doors that can be locked. Each room has its own key to unlock only its door. There is, however, a master key that will unlock any door in the complex. I think about this master key when I meditate on the presence of God.

You see, in the Word of God there are various "keys" to cover various situations. There is one key to unlock healing, another key to deliverance, another to abundance, another to relationships. But there is also a master key which will unlock all of these and provide anything else that belongs to the believer. This master key is the presence of God.

When you are living and walking in the presence of Almighty God, sickness has to go. No disease can withstand His presence.

When you live in His presence, poverty and insufficiency

must flee. There can be no lack in the presence of the God who made heaven and earth.

Every promise found in the Word of God is wrapped up and available in His sweet presence. It truly is the master key.

## The Moving Presence

One of the first things you must recognize about the presence of God is that it isn't just a place you come to visit. It moves with you wherever you go.

Listen to God's words to Moses:

> My *presence shall go with thee, and I will give thee rest.*

> Exodus 33:14

Did you catch that? God said to him, "My presence shall go with thee." The presence of God, with all the power and peace it brings, can go with you wherever you go. You can carry it to work or to the grocery store.

The presence of God ought to be such a tangible part of who you are that people will notice something different about you. They will say to themselves, *I don't know what it is, but there's something powerful about that person.* That's the presence of the God of the universe with you and in you.

## *The Benefit of Rest*

As the title of this book suggests, there are many benefits associated with the presence of God. The last Scripture verse we read names one of these benefits: *rest*.

The presence of God is where your struggling and striving ends. When you live in His presence, you no longer have to sweat and strain in your own ability. God is your Covenant Partner and you are operating in the power of His anointing.

Remember when Adam fell and brought the curse upon himself? Part of the curse involved hard, difficult work and sweat. The Scripture says:

> *. . . cursed is the ground for thy sake; in sorrow shalt thou eat of it all the days of thy life;*
>
> *Thorns also and thistles shall it bring forth to thee; and thou shalt eat the herb of the field;*
>
> *In the sweat of thy face shalt thou eat bread, till thou return unto the ground. . . .*
>
> Genesis 3:17–19

In Jesus we have been redeemed from the curse of the Law. In the presence of God we have rest. Praise God!

When you live in the presence of God, you don't have to be racked with worry about how you are going to pay your bills. You don't have to be tormented by depression, guilt, or fear. Jesus said:

> *Come unto me, all ye that labour and are heavy laden, and I will give you rest.*
>
> *Take my yoke upon you, and learn of me; for I am meek and lowly in heart: and ye shall find rest unto your souls.*

Matthew 11:28,29

When you get into the presence of the Lord, you will find rest and will discover that the struggle is over.

When you are walking in that kind of rest, you will get other people's attention. Some will think you have a problem; others may think you're crazy. People will be saying: "Don't you realize what you're up against? Don't you understand the kind of challenge you're facing? You should be worried!"

But you will respond to them: "No, I've got the master key. When I got up this morning, I entered into the presence of God, and His presence has gone with me all through this day. There's rest in the presence of God. I can rest because I know that in His presence all my needs are met."

Yes, there is rest in the presence of the living God. But that isn't all you will find. There's more, much more.

## *The Benefit of Glory and Honor*

Take a look at a portion of 1 Chronicles 16:27:

*Glory and honour are in his presence. . . .*

Many Christians have no idea what the "glory" of God really is. They think of it only as a mysterious cloud that appeared from time to time in the Old Testament.

Actually, the God-kind of glory appears any time something promised in the Word is manifested in the physical realm. For instance, when healing, as promised in the Word, comes into someone's life, that's glory. When supernatural provision is manifested, that's glory.

Where can you go to see the glory of God manifested in your life? According to the verse we just read, that glory comes when you enter into the presence of God. It also says glory has a partner: honor. What kind of honor? The honor of God.

Honor and glory go hand in hand. We see them linked in Psalm 8:5 (AMP):

*Yet You have made him [man] but a little lower than God . . . and You have crowned him with glory and honor.*

Don't make the mistake of thinking that you ever have any honor or glory of your own. It's when you dwell in the presence of God that His honor and His glory are imparted to you. You can't be around God without His nature rubbing off on you.

We see honor linked to the presence of God in Psalm 91. This psalm is all about the benefits that come from dwelling in "the shadow of the Almighty" (v. 1); in other words, from living in the presence of God.

The last two verses of this psalm actually tell us that God wants to honor us!

> *He shall call upon me, and I will answer him:* **I will be with him** *in trouble;* **I will deliver him,** *and honour him.*
>
> *With long life will I satisfy him, and shew him my salvation.*
>
> Psalm 91:15,16

According to verse 15, in the presence of the Lord comes honor, and with honor comes deliverance from trouble. That's what I call a benefit!

## A Source of Strength

A few paragraphs back, we looked at a portion of 1 Chronicles 16:27. There we saw that glory and honor are to be found in the presence of God. Let's look at this entire verse:

*Glory and honour are in his presence; strength and
gladness are in his place.*

Think about that. Strength and gladness are in the place
where God is. I don't know about you, but there have been
quite a few days in my life when a little strength and gladness
would have come in mighty handy!

When you need to be strengthened, you will find it in the
presence of the Lord. When feelings of sadness, discourage-
ment, or oppression try to move in on your mind, you will find
gladness in His presence, too.

That's why it is so vital that we invest our time in reading
God's Word, meditating on it, and fellowshipping with the
Lord in prayer. These four vital resources for successful living
are found there in God's presence: glory, honor, strength, and
gladness.

## The Benefit of Joy

Maybe you know the verse in Nehemiah 8:10 which states,
". . . for the joy of the Lord is your strength." This Scripture
has been quoted many times. But most people don't know how
to receive the joy of the Lord when they need it.

It doesn't do you any good to know that the joy of the Lord
is your strength if you don't also know how to access some of
that joy when times are tough. You can't just work up this joy
in your own flesh.

The key to tapping into the source of joy is found in the sixteenth psalm:

> *Thou wilt shew me the path of life:* **in thy presence is fulness of joy;** *at thy right hand there are pleasures for evermore.*

Psalm 16:11

As you may have guessed, in the presence of God you will find the kind of joy that will give you supernatural strength. How much joy can you find in the presence of the Lord? All you can hold. As this Scripture verse says, you will find "*fulness* of joy."

If you need strength to get your bills paid, to come out of depression, or to overcome an attack on your health, you will find this strength abundantly in God's presence.

You see, we have been looking for answers in all the wrong places.

Everything you need, everything you desire, everything God wants to give you—all this can be found in His presence.

## Claim Your Benefits!

Thou wilt shew me the path of life: in thy presence is fullness of joy; at thy right hand there are pleasures for evermore.

Psalm 16:11

## My prayer in the power of the Word . . .

_____

_____

_____

_____

_____

_____

_____

## Study Questions

1. Describe someone you know who clearly has the presence of God with them.

_____

_____

_____

_____

_____

2. Why is rest important to God's people?

_____

_____

_____

_____

_____

3. Where do you see the glory of God manifested in your own life?

_____

_____

_____

_____

_____

4. What does it mean that "the joy of the Lord is my strength"?

_____

_____

_____

_____

_____

# The Path to God's Presence

To this point in this study, we have spent most of our time examining the benefits of abiding in the presence of God and how the mercy of God makes His presence available to us.

Now it's time to discover *how* to get into God's presence and stay there. It doesn't do you any good to know how wonderful the presence of the Lord is if you don't know how to get there.

Let's begin with some general guidelines for moving into the presence of the Lord.

## Thanksgiving

First, we should be asking ourselves, *What does the Word have to say on the subject of God's presence?* Let's look at Psalm 95 to find the answer.

*Let us come before his presence with thanksgiving, and*
*make a joyful noise unto him with psalms.*

Psalm 95:2

This verse contains two key elements that bring us into the presence of God. The first is *thanksgiving*. Thanksgiving escorts us into the presence of God like nothing else can.

The first thing I do during my prayer times with the Lord is to spend a few moments thanking Him for all He has done for me. This never fails to usher me into God's presence. It also focuses my attention on the goodness and faithfulness of God rather than on my problems.

If, instead of complaining, you will spend some time thanking God for all the things He does for you, you will find yourself in the right frame of mind to enter God's presence.

## Praise

The second element to successfully entering the presence of God is *praise*. We see this in the last part of the verse we just read from Psalm 95:

. . . *make a joyful noise unto him with psalms.*

Psalm 95:2

Praise is similar to thanksgiving but not the same. Thanks-giving honors God for *what He has done*. Praise honors Him for *who He is*.

To bring God on the scene, you have to start praising Him. As Psalm 22:3 says, God inhabits the praises of His people.

## *Make a Joyful Noise!*

We see both of these elements, *thanksgiving* and *praise*, in the familiar Psalm 100. This psalm almost draws us a road map to the throne of God.

> *Make a joyful noise unto the Lord, all ye lands.*
> *Serve the Lord with gladness: come before his pres-ence with singing.*

> Psalm 100:1,2

Here we see one of the two elements we have already iden-tified. The joyful noise we are to make represents praise. We are to come before His presence with singing.

You may not be able to carry a tune, but you should be singing a song of praise to the Lord from your heart. He will honor that by filling your heart and your room with the sweet-ness of His presence.

During biblical times, if you were entering the temple in Jerusalem, you would come first to the gates. After passing through those gates, you would enter the courts. Then and only then would you be prepared to enter the Holy Place where the presence of the Lord dwelt (but only if you were the high priest). This is the imagery we can see in this psalm:

> Enter into his **gates** with thanksgiving, and into his **courts** with praise: be thankful unto him, and bless his name.
>
> Psalm 100:4

Here we see these two vital elements together—*thanksgiving* and *praise*. We are told that thanksgiving will get you through the gates and praise will take you through the courts.

What is it that takes you the rest of the way into God's presence? Our old friends, *goodness* and *mercy*.

> For the Lord is good; his mercy is everlasting; and his truth endureth to all generations.
>
> Psalm 100:5

Now let's get practical and specific about *how* you are to cultivate the presence of the Lord in your life. There are actually several avenues available to you for reaching the presence of God and living in His presence. Any of them will get you there, but all of them are important.

## *The Word*

We have made reference to this principle throughout this book. Now it's time to just lay it out, plain and simple.

By getting into God's Word, you are entering into His presence. God is His Word.

> *In the beginning was the Word, and the Word was with*
> *God, and the Word was God.*

John 1:1

God and His Word are inseparable. When you open the Bible with a heart to see and hear God, you won't be disappointed.

You simply can't be exposed to the presence of God through His Word without being changed. It will affect you. It will change your thought patterns and your habits. It will change your desires, your attitudes, the way you look at things.

The reality is, no one can *force* you into the presence of God. You have to make that choice yourself; no one can make it for you. To reap the benefits of His presence, you have to make a quality decision to spend time in God's Word on a regular basis. I don't mean throwing your Bible open for a few

102

minutes every now and then while you keep one eye on your television. I mean making a commitment to set aside concentrated quality time in the Word.

This is what separates the powerful, victorious Christians from the "wannabes"—those who want to experience victory but don't want to pay the price.

You can't give yourself to every influence and activity under the sun, while dedicating only a few token moments a week to God's Word, and still expect to walk in victory and power. It simply won't happen.

You have to make up your mind to get into the Word.

You also need to get involved in a church where God's Word is being taught uncompromisingly. You can't sit under teaching that's filled with religious tradition, doubt, and unbelief, and expect to experience the presence of God on a regular basis. The bad teaching you receive will inevitably come out of you when the pressure is on. Find a church with a pastor who preaches the Word and sit under that teaching every opportunity you can.

Start letting the Word of God change your thinking. As Romans 12:2 says, ". . . be ye transformed by the renewing of your mind. . . ." Renew your mind with the Word of God. This is a powerful way to experience His presence.

## *Prayer*

Another way to experience the presence of God is through prayer.

I'm not talking about the "Now I lay me down to sleep" kind of praying practiced by some believers. I'm talking about moving into a realm where you and God talk to each other as intimate friends.

Prayer isn't to be just a monologue, with you conducting a one-way transmission of your needs to God. Prayer is communication. It's give and take, talking and listening, fellowshipping.

There are many types of prayers, but one of the most powerful and most effective involves praying God's Word. As was previously pointed out, God's Word ushers us into His presence. So, what could be more powerful than praying the Word?

God's Word is His will. His will is in His Word. If you are praying what God's Word says, you can know beyond all doubt that you are praying in accordance with the will of God.

## *Giving Thanks*

We have already touched on this. Giving thanks brings us into the presence of God. As Psalm 100 says, we enter into His courts with thanksgiving.

This is why the apostle Paul said:

*Pray without ceasing.*
   *In every thing give thanks: for this is the will of God in Christ Jesus concerning you.*

1 Thessalonians 5:17,18

Paul knew that thanksgiving would usher us into the presence of God and that His presence is the master key to all the promises of God.

## Claim Your Benefits!

Let us come before his presence with thanksgiving, and make a joyful noise unto him with psalms.

Psalm 95:2

## My prayer in the power of the Word . . .

_____

_____

_____

_____

_____

_____

_____

## Study Questions

1. Spend a few moments offering words of thanksgiving to God for all He has done.

_____

_____

_____

_____

_____

2. Next, spend some time praising His name for who He is.

_____

_____

_____

_____

_____

3. Take a few minutes to read through John chapter 1 in order to view Christ as the Word.

_____

_____

_____

_____

_____

4. End this session by taking time to talk with God in prayer. Make sure to listen as well as speak.

_____

_____

_____

_____

_____

# 10

## *Those Who Benefit from the Presence of God*

GOD IS NO respecter of persons; His presence is available to every believer. The newest baby Christian has just as much access to the throne room of God as the apostle Paul did.

The fact remains, however, that only a few believers enjoy the many benefits that come from living in God's presence, while the vast majority live very much like the rest of the world. What's the difference?

A careful examination of Scripture will show us that the people who consistently experience the presence of God have certain characteristics in common. Join me as we explore God's Word for the traits of those who benefit from the presence of God.

## *Boldness*

One of the main symbols of the presence of God in Scripture is the Holy of Holies, or the Holy Place.

As we saw in the previous chapter, the tabernacle of God was divided into three segments: the outer courts, the inner court, and, finally, the Holy Place.

The Holy Place was where the ark of the covenant was kept. The ark represented God's presence in Israel. Only the high priest was permitted to enter the Holy Place, and then only once a year.

Entering the Holy Place was most serious for the high priest. Before he entered it, the other priests attached a bell to his robe and tied a rope around his ankle. (See Ex. 28:34,35.) The tinkling of the bell let them know the high priest was still alive as he performed his duties in the Holy Place.

Bearing all this in mind makes Hebrews 10:19 sound downright shocking:

> *Having therefore, brethren, boldness to enter into the holiest by the blood of Jesus. . . .*

What is God saying here? He is telling us that, in Jesus, we can enter the Holy Place where the presence of God is; and we can do it, not with fear and trembling, but with boldness!

What gives us the right to enter God's presence with such boldness? The blood of Jesus. His blood cleanses us and sanc-

tifies us, making us as worthy to enter God's presence as Jesus
Himself.

> But now in Christ Jesus ye who sometimes were far off
> are **made nigh by the blood of Christ.**

Ephesians 2:13

> But if we walk in the light, as he is in the light, we have
> fellowship one with another, **and the blood of Jesus
> Christ his Son cleanseth us from all sin.**

1 John 1:7

> And from Jesus Christ, who is the faithful witness, and
> the first begotten of the dead, and the prince of the
> kings of the earth. Unto him that loved us, and
> **washed us from our sins in his own blood. . . .**

Revelation 1:5

When I go into my prayer closet, one of the first things I do
is thank God for the blood of Jesus. I say:

> Father, I thank You for the blood of Jesus. I thank You
> that by His blood, I have the right to enter Your pres-
> ence. I thank You that through His blood I have for-

*giveness of sin. I thank You that the blood of Jesus cleanses me from all unrighteousness and from an evil conscience. I thank You that because of the blood of Jesus I am successful in everything I do.*

When you praise and thank God for the blood of Jesus, boldness begins to rise up within you. You gain the confidence to enter the Holy Place by reminding yourself of what Jesus' blood has done to you and for you.

This boldness is one of the key characteristics of those who abide in the presence of God.

## ⌐ A Lifestyle of Praise

Another trait you will almost always see in someone who enjoys the many benefits of living in God's presence is a lifestyle of praise.

People whose first instinct in any crisis is to praise God are people who have instant access to the delivering presence of God. We see a classic example of this in Acts, chapter 16, when Paul and Silas were in prison:

*And when they had laid many stripes upon them, they cast them into prison, charging the jailor to keep them safely:*

*Who, having received such a charge, thrust them into the inner prison, and made their feet fast in the stocks.*

*And at midnight Paul and Silas prayed,* **and sang praises unto God:** *and the prisoners heard them.*

Acts 16:23–25

Put yourself in Paul's place for a moment. You have just been falsely accused, beaten viciously with a whip, and thrown into a dark sewer of a dungeon with irons cutting into your legs. Would your first instinct be to sing some praise songs? Probably not. But that's what Paul and Silas did.

How did God respond to their songs of praise?

*And suddenly there was a great earthquake, so that the foundations of the prison were shaken: and immediately all the doors were opened, and every one's bands were loosed.*

Acts 16:26

Notice that Paul's deliverance came suddenly. That's the nature of praise. It will bring God into your situation instantly.

You may be in a different kind of prison today. You may be imprisoned by debt, by alcohol, by sickness, or by fear. If you will stay in God's presence through praise, you will find God showing Himself strong on your behalf to break you out of that situation.

## *Stewardship*

There is still another characteristic you will almost always see in the lives of people who enjoy the benefits of God's presence. Their money is always at God's disposal. In other words, they are good stewards of what God has entrusted to them.

We see this illustrated in the life of a man named Cornelius in Acts, chapter 10. Notice what the Word says about this Gentile centurion:

> *There was a certain man in Caesarea called Cornelius, a centurion of the band called the Italian band,*
>
> *A devout man, and one that feared God with all his house, which **gave much alms to the people,** and prayed to God alway.*
>
> *He saw in a vision evidently about the ninth hour of the day an angel of God coming in to him, and saying unto him, Cornelius.*
>
> *And when he looked on him, he was afraid, and said, What is it, Lord? And he said unto him, **Thy prayers and thine alms are come up for a memorial before God.***

Acts 10:1–4

We are reading about a very historical event here. God was looking for a Gentile to be the first non-Jew who is born again.

To that point, everyone believing on Jesus had been Jewish. It had not even occurred to Peter that a Gentile *could* be born again.

So when God set out to find the man who would be the first of millions upon millions of Gentile believers, who did He choose? A man whose prayers and alms had gone up as a memorial before Him.

*Alms* refers to giving to the poor and to the work of God. God is looking for people to bless who can own money without money owning them.

How do you demonstrate your faithfulness with finances? Simple: by tithing and giving offerings. It got God's attention in the case of Cornelius, and it will get His attention in your case, too.

God is looking for faithful stewards—people He can entrust with fortunes and wealth, knowing they will distribute it wherever He tells them.

Show me someone who is enjoying the many benefits of God's presence, and I will show you someone who tithes and gives as the Spirit leads.

## Fearlessness

Let me bring your attention to one more characteristic of those who enjoy God's presence: freedom from fear.

Without exception, people who spend time with God on a regular basis don't experience much fear or anxiety. Why?

An entire psalm is devoted to this truth. Look with me at Psalm 91:

> *He that dwelleth in the secret place of the most High*
> *shall abide under the shadow of the Almighty.*
>
> Psalm 91:1

This verse is describing someone who lives (or abides) in the presence of God. The secret place is that place of intimate prayer and fellowship with God.

The next few verses of this psalm tell us what kind of outlook such a person would have:

> *I will say of the Lord, He is my refuge and my fortress:*
> *my God; in him will I trust.*
>
> *Surely he shall deliver thee from the snare of the*
> *fowler, and from the noisome pestilence.*
>
> *He shall cover thee with his feathers, and under his*
> *wings shalt thou trust: his truth shall be thy shield and*
> *buckler.*
>
> *Thou shalt not be afraid for the terror by night; nor*
> *for the arrow that flieth by day;*
>
> *Nor for the pestilence that walketh in darkness; nor*
> *for the destruction that wasteth at noonday.*
>
> Psalm 91:2–6

The person who lives daily in fellowship with God knows no fear. He can walk in the quiet confidence which comes from knowing that nothing in hell or on earth can touch him. Nothing the enemy throws at him can penetrate the protecting shield of God's presence.

The rest of this psalm describes the supernatural protection such a person enjoys:

*A thousand shall fall at thy side, and ten thousand at thy right hand; but it shall not come nigh thee.*

*Only with thine eyes shalt thou behold and see the reward of the wicked.*

*Because thou hast made the Lord, which is my refuge, even the most High, thy habitation;*

*There shall no evil befall thee, neither shall any plague come nigh thy dwelling.*

*For he shall give his angels charge over thee, to keep thee in all thy ways.*

*They shall bear thee up in their hands, lest thou dash thy foot against a stone.*

*Thou shalt tread upon the lion and adder: the young lion and the dragon shalt thou trample under feet.*

*Because he hath set his love upon me, therefore will I deliver him: I will set him on high, because he hath known my name.*

*He shall call upon me, and I will answer him: I will be with him in trouble; I will deliver him, and honour him.*

*With long life will I satisfy him, and shew him my salvation.*

Psalm 91:7–16

Fearlessness—the surefire indicator of a person who knows and walks in the presence of the Lord.

## God's Presence Throughout History

For thousands of years now, the presence of God has been empowering men and women who would pay the price to press into it.

When Adam knew the presence of God, all his needs were met beyond his wildest dreams. His every need was anticipated and supplied in abundance.

When Noah experienced the presence of God, he gained the instruction and wisdom to build an ark. That ark saved a remnant of the human race. (Gen. 6.)

We are told that Moses talked to God man to man, like a man talks with his friend. Moses knew the presence of God, and through it he gained the power to bring down kingdoms, split seas, and bring water from a rock. (Ex. 3:1–10; 14:15–31; 17:5,6.)

When the presence of God was upon Samson, he wielded the strength of a hundred men. (Judg. 15:14,15.)

David—the shepherd, psalmist, and king—knew the presence of the Lord. Through it he gained the power to bring down giants, slay tens of thousands in battle, and be declared "a man after mine [God's] own heart." (1 Sam. 17:32–51; 18:7; Acts 13:22.)

Solomon, in the presence of God, gained legendary wisdom—wisdom to build one of the richest kingdoms the earth has ever known. (1 Kings 3:9–14.)

Isaiah experienced the presence of the Lord. He saw the Lord "high and lifted up, and his train filled the temple" (Isa. 6:1). He described the Spirit of the Lord resting upon Him as "the spirit of wisdom and understanding, the spirit of counsel and might, the spirit of knowledge and of the fear of the Lord" (Isa. 11:2).

Jeremiah described the presence of the Lord as "a burning fire shut up in my bones" (Jer. 20:9).

Esther knew the presence of the Lord. She saw God give her favor and elevate her in order to save all of God's people in her country from certain death. (Est. 2:17; 7:1–6.)

Job experienced the presence of the Lord and through it gained understanding. Everything he had lost was restored many times over. (Job 42:10–17.)

Daniel, in the presence of the Lord, saw deliverance from the mouths of hungry lions. (Dan. 6:16–23.)

Throughout history, men and women who have made a quality decision to press in to the presence of the Lord have reaped the benefits. But not everyone in the Bible made the right decision.

## *Running from the Presence of God*

There is a flip side to this coin we have been examining. Just as there are benefits that come from pressing into the presence of God, there are also penalties incurred for running from it.

The classic biblical example of someone who ran from God's presence is Jonah. Look with me at his story:

> *Now the word of the Lord came unto Jonah the son of Amittai, saying,*
>
> *Arise, go to Nineveh, that great city, and cry against it; for their wickedness is come up before me.*
>
> ***But Jonah rose up to flee** unto Tarshish **from the presence of the Lord,** and went down to Joppa; and he found a ship going to Tarshish: so he paid the fare thereof, and went down into it, to go with them unto Tarshish from the presence of the Lord.*
>
> Jonah 1:1–3

Jonah, as a prophet of God, should have known better. He should have been aware that staying in the will and presence of the Lord is where the benefits are. But, like all of us do from time to time, Jonah decided he had a better handle on the situation than God did. Instead of obeying and staying under the protection of God's shadow, he took off in another direction.

As a child of God, don't ever move out from under God's umbrella of protection. Don't ever move out of the secret place of the Most High. It's dangerous out there! Whenever you run away from God, you're on your own. Jonah discovered this in a hurry.

> But the Lord sent out [allowed] a great wind into the sea, and there was a mighty tempest in the sea, so that the ship was like to be broken.
>
> Jonah 1:4

When, out of rebellion or disobedience, you flee from the presence of God, you will experience the opposite of all the benefits we have been talking about in this study. Instead of provision, you will experience lack. Instead of peace and security, you will experience fear. Instead of health, you will open yourself to every vile thing the enemy tries to put on you.

Living in the presence of God has many benefits. And, as Gloria Copeland says, neglecting it is just plain stupid.

## Claim Your Benefits!

But if we walk in the light, as he is in the light, we have fellowship one with another, and the blood of Jesus Christ his Son cleanseth us from all sin.

1 John 1:7

## My prayer in the power of the Word . . .

_____

_____

_____

_____

_____

_____

_____

## Study Questions

1. Whom do you know whom you'd describe as a bold Christian? What makes him or her that way?

_____

_____

_____

_____

_____

2. Whom do you know who has a life filled with praise? What would you say is the difference praise makes in his or her life?

_____

_____

_____

_____

_____

3. Who is the most generous Christian you know? What impact has his or her generosity had in the world?

_____

_____

_____

_____

_____

4. Who is the most fearless believer you've ever met? How does the presence of God make us fearless?

_____

_____

_____

_____

_____

11

# God's Plan to Regain Man's Coat of Glory

AT ONE LEVEL, this book is obviously about the presence of God and all the good things that come from living in it. But it's really about more than that.

At a deeper level, this is the story of God's plan of the ages—a plan designed to regain for man the coat of glory which Adam forfeited in the Garden.

On a personal level, it's a story about the mind-boggling opportunity you have to fellowship with the Creator of heaven and earth. To talk with Him. To get His counsel. To draw on His wisdom. As the apostle Paul said, to really know Him. (Phil. 3:10.)

In closing this study, I believe it would be beneficial for us to step back and get the big picture of this remarkable story.

## *The Coat of Glory*

As we have seen, prior to the Fall, man was equipped to fellowship with God with perfect ease. Adam and Eve would walk with God in the cool of the day, enjoying His company.

According to Psalm 8:5, God had made man just a little lower than Himself and had "crowned him with glory and honour." In other words, man was literally *clothed* in the glory of God. This explains why Adam and Eve didn't know they were naked until after they had sinned. Their rebellion and fall caused that covering of glory to be removed.

When this happened, two things became evident to Adam and Eve.

First, they saw that they were naked and needed to cover themselves. As the Scripture says:

> *And the eyes of them both were opened, and they knew that they were naked; and they sewed fig leaves together, and made themselves aprons.*

> Genesis 3:7

Second, they were no longer able to walk and talk with God with the intimacy and naturalness as they had in the past.

> *And they heard the voice of the Lord God walking in the garden in the cool of the day: and Adam and his*

*wife hid themselves from the presence of the Lord God*
*amongst the trees of the garden.*

Genesis 3:8

Without this covering of glory, there was no way they could stand in the holiness of God's presence and survive—and they knew it.

From that point on, the Bible is essentially the unfolding of God's plan to restore to man the glory cloak that had been lost. Why was this so important to God? Because, as hard as it is for us to comprehend, God values our fellowship. He missed the level of intimacy He had enjoyed with Adam.

What a wonderful and mysterious truth! God desires our company. And He was willing to send His Son, right at that critical moment in history, to restore us to fellowship with Him.

## Jesus, the Word Made Flesh

As we have seen previously, the entrance of Jesus into the earth represented the critical point in God's master plan to restore man to fellowship with Himself.

Jesus was literally God in a suit of flesh, just like yours and mine. As we have seen in John 1, He is "the Word."

*And the Word was made flesh, and dwelt among us,*
*(and we beheld his glory, the glory as of the only be-*
*gotten of the Father,) full of grace and truth.*

John 1:14

127

## *Two-Part Plan for Man: Redeemed and Adopted*

The Bible is very clear. God wanted man restored to fellowship with Him. This required a two-part plan. The first part called for Jesus to redeem us. The second part called for God's Holy Spirit to give us a spirit of adoption so that we would once more feel at home in God's presence.

We see this two-part plan described in Galatians, chapter 4:

> *But when the fulness of the time was come, God sent forth his Son, made of a woman, made under the law,*
>
> *To redeem them that were under the law, that we might receive the adoption of sons.*
>
> *And because ye are sons, God hath sent forth the Spirit of his Son into your hearts, crying, Abba, Father.*
>
> *Wherefore thou art no more a servant, but a son; and if a son, then an heir of God through Christ.*
>
> Galatians 4:4–7

The second phase of this plan became a reality when God poured out His Spirit upon all those who would receive it. It is this indwelling and infilling of the Holy Ghost that

128

gives us the ability to fellowship in God's presence like no one has been able to do since Adam's fall.

> *For as many as are led by the Spirit of God, they are the sons of God.*
>
> *For ye have not received the spirit of bondage again to fear; but ye have received the Spirit of adoption, whereby we cry, Abba, Father.*
>
> *The Spirit itself beareth witness with our spirit, that we are the children of God:*
>
> *And if children, then heirs; heirs of God, and joint-heirs with Christ; if so be that we suffer with him, that we may be also glorified together.*
>
> Romans 8:14–17

Because of the Spirit of God living and moving within us, we no longer have to shrink back in fear and shame from the presence of God. We now have something called *access*.

> *For through him we both have access by one Spirit unto the Father.*
>
> Ephesians 2:18

## *Regaining the Coat*

At this point you may be wondering, "So what remains to be done? When do we regain this coat of glory?"

The answer is twofold. We progressively regain the former glory as we spend time in the presence of God. Hanging out with God transforms us into His image!

> *But we all, with open face beholding as in a glass the glory of the Lord, are changed into the same image from glory to glory, even as by the Spirit of the Lord.*

2 Corinthians 3:18

We are being changed into His image, but complete restoration will not occur this side of heaven. This restoration of all Adam possessed will take place the moment we are instantly transformed at the coming of the Lord Jesus Christ.

> *Behold, I shew you a mystery; We shall not all sleep, but we shall all be changed,*
>
> *In a moment, in the twinkling of an eye, at the last trump: for the trumpet shall sound, and the dead shall be raised incorruptible, and we shall be changed.*
>
> *For this corruptible must put on incorruption, and this mortal must put on immortality.*

1 Corinthians 15:51–53

I am convinced that this day is not far off. I believe with all my heart that the signs of the times indicate Jesus is coming back for His Bride very soon.

Until then, you have the privilege of fellowshipping and communing with God on a daily basis. As you do, you will be transformed from glory to glory, and you will be ready for Him when He comes!

## Claim Your Benefits!

For as many as are led by the Spirit of God, they are the sons of God.
For ye have not received the spirit of bondage again to fear; but ye have received the Spirit of adoption, whereby we cry, Abba, Father.

Romans 8:14,15

## My prayer in the power of the Word . . .

_____

_____

_____

_____

_____

_____

# Study Questions

1. What would you say is God's plan for mankind?

_____

_____

_____

_____

_____

2. In your own words, what happened when Adam and Eve chose to sin?

_____

_____

_____

_____

_____

3. How does the redemptive work of Jesus Christ change things in the world?

_____

_____

_____

_____

_____

4. What difference does it make in your life to know that you've been adopted as one of God's children?

_____

_____

_____

_____

_____

# 12

# *Claiming Your Benefits*

*T*HE GLORIOUS, WONDROUS, *awesome presence of God.*

What an amazing thing it is to realize that in Jesus you have the right to enter into His presence.

It's even more astounding to think that God *desires* your presence. He has gone to extraordinary lengths to make available to you access to His presence.

What a tragedy it is that so few believers exercise this right. If only more believers knew of the benefits of God's presence.

In His presence you will find peace.

In His presence you will find strength.

In His presence you will find an abundance—everything you could possibly ever need.

Do you want your needs met? Do you want to prosper financially, physically, and in your relationships? Then get into God's presence.

This is the master key to everything you could ever want or dream of. It is the key to healing, the key to increase, the key to promotion.

Make a quality decision to take hold of that key today. Purpose in your heart to turn off your television, get before God, and spend time in His Word.

Once you taste it, you will never go back to living the way you did before. You will never go back to living without those benefits that come from being in God's presence.

## Claim Your Benefits!

In the beginning was the Word, and the Word was with God, and the Word was God.

John 1:1

## My prayer in the power of the Word . . .

_____

_____

_____

_____

_____

_____

_____

## Study Questions

1. What has been the most important lesson you learned in this study?

_____

_____

_____

_____

_____

2. What verse of Scripture stands out to you from your time with this book?

_____

_____

_____

_____

_____

3. What do you believe God is doing in your life right now?

_____

_____

_____

_____

_____

4. Take the time to pray and ask God to help you apply these truths today.

_____

_____

_____

_____

_____

# Endnotes

## Chapter 1

1. Strong, James H. "Hebrew and Chaldee Dictionary," in *Strong's Exhaustive Concordance* (Grand Rapids: Baker, 1992), 12.
2. ———. *Strong's Exhaustive Concordance* (Grand Rapids: Baker, 1992), 397–406.
3. ———. "Greek Dictionary of the New Testament," in *Strong's Exhaustive Concordance* (Grand Rapids: Baker, 1992), 35.

## Chapter 4

1. Strong, James H. "Hebrew and Chaldee Dictionary," in *Strong's Exhaustive Concordance* (Grand Rapids: Baker, 1992), 41.
2. ———. "Hebrew and Chaldee Dictionary," in *Strong's Exhaustive Concordance* (Grand Rapids: Baker, 1992), 107.

# *About the Author*

DR. CREFLO A. DOLLAR is the founder and senior pastor of World Changers Church International (WCCI) in College Park, Georgia, and World Changers Church-New York. With 20 years of experience in ministry, Dr. Dollar is committed to bringing the Good News of Jesus Christ to people all over the world, literally changing the world one person at a time.

A former educational therapist, Dr. Dollar received the vision for World Changers in 1986. He held the church's first worship service in the cafeteria of Kathleen Mitchell Elementary School in College Park with only eight people in attendance. Over the years the ministry grew rapidly, and the congregation moved from the cafeteria to a modest-sized chapel, adding a weekly radio broadcast and four services each Sunday. On December 24, 1995, WCCI moved into its present location, the 8,500–seat sanctuary known as the World Dome. At a cost of nearly $20 million, the World Dome was built without any bank financing. The construction of the World Dome is a testament to the miracle-working power of

God and remains a model of debt-freedom that ministries all over the world emulate.

A native of College Park, Dr. Dollar received his bachelor's degree in educational therapy from West Georgia College and was awarded a Doctor of Divinity degree from Oral Roberts University in 1998. He is the publisher of *CHANGE*, an international quarterly lifestyle magazine with over 100,000 subscribers that gives Christians the tools they need to experience total life prosperity. His award-winning *Changing Your World* television broadcast reaches nearly one billion homes in practically every country in the world. A much sought-after conference speaker and author, Dr. Dollar is known for his practical approach to the Bible and has encouraged thousands to pursue a personal relationship with God. Dr. Dollar and his wife, Taffi, have five children and live in Atlanta.

# Books by Dr. Creflo A. Dollar

*In the Presence of God*
*Live Without Fear*
*Not Guilty*
*Love, Live, and Enjoy Life*
*Breaking Out of Trouble*
*Walking in the Confidence of God in Troubled Times*